Female Ensemble

Project Manager: **Carol Cuellar**
Art Design: **Olivia D. Novak**
Photography: **Joan Marcus**

Female Ensemble

Michael Arnold and Company

Jonathan Freeman and Mary Testa

David Elder, Christine Ebersole
and Female Ensemble

C O N T E N T S

This is April 2, 1933, and today we start work on a new show. We're going to rehearse four weeks, then try out in Atlantic City. We're going to rehearse 12 hours a day, seven days a week. You're going to dance till your feet fall off and you aren't able to stand up. But five weeks from today, Pretty Lady *is going to be the best damned show this town has ever seen. You're on your way to glory—and 32 bucks a week!"*

Once more, the call to arms—and legs—is heard on Broadway. In a voice raspy from a parched period of flop shows, Julian Marsh, the once-famous director, is issuing marching orders to a troop of chorines, whipping them into a frenzy of show-biz sell.

With pep talk like that, *42nd Street*, winner of the 2001 Tony Award for Best Revival of a Musical, picks up precisely where *A Chorus Line* left off and perpetuates the archetypal Backstage Musical another round, all the way up to opening night. Broadway's two longest-running American musicals tell the same tale; it's just that *42nd Street* throws a wider net than *A Chorus Line*'s small camp of gypsies.

Bradford Ropes created the cliché in a 1928 novel. Busby Berkeley crystallized it into geometric designs for the movies in 1933, to the timeless tunes of Al Dubin and Harry Warren. And David Merrick transplanted it to its original setting—Broadway—in 1980.

Now, 20 seasons later, director Mark Bramble and choreographer Randy Skinner are going for perfect symmetry by plopping their *42nd Street* down right square on 42nd Street, of all probable places, at the massive Ford Center for the Performing Arts.

Both find the experience more than *déjà vu*. Bramble co-authored the original book for the show with Michael Stewart; Skinner, along with Karin Baker, assisted Gower Champion in choreographing the show. They remember it well, very well.

On Aug. 25, 1980, *42nd Street* had one of Broadway's most memorable openings—not because the cast had knocked the show over the balcony and out of the park (it would run eight-and-a-half years; 3,486 performances) but because of the news producer Merrick brought center stage after the curtain call: that Champion had died hours before.

Bramble and Skinner were among the few informed before the show of Champion's passing. The cast and the customers were not informed until Merrick's pronouncement, and, even then—given his famous flair for flashy showmanship—it was hard to take him at his word.

"That was a very hard experience to go through," recalls Bramble. "We didn't know that Gower was that ill. Later, we found out that his doctor had told him he would probably not survive the project. He had told Gower to return to California, walk on the beach and enjoy the rest of his time—but that just wasn't Gower. He got his life in California organized and moved into a sublet apartment in New York, knowing that he might not survive—and, indeed, he didn't."

Skinner recalls gradually becoming aware of Champion's illness: "I knew it when we got to Washington, D.C. because he was hospitalized several times during the out-of-town tryout. His energy level was down, but he didn't open up and talk about any of that. Later [in previews], he said he'd been told his illness could be hastened by being up dancing a lot or expending energy or stress. And putting on a Broadway musical—is there anything more stressful in life? It was one of those double-edged swords where you try to do the thing you love yet you don't feel well. . . . So you can imagine what it'd be like to work on a big dance show and not feel at your peak."

"Several months after the opening night," says Bramble, "David Merrick and I were going to dinner, and David said—this is a direct quote: 'Gower Champion staged his exit perfectly, and no one could have promoted it better than David Merrick.' Which, of course, is true. He got the front page of *The New York Times* three days in a row. I don't think that any show in the history of the American theatre has had that."

Although he did go on to produce other shows, *42nd Street* was basically Merrick's last great hurrah, too. "He played it like a fiddle," Bramble remembers with a smile. "He manipulated the New York press, the audience. He manipulated us all.

"He had been in Hollywood for a while at that time, and he told me, 'I hate the movies. I can't be in charge. No one person can be in charge on a movie.' He wanted to come back to Broadway and throw his weight around. In fact, we had trouble raising money for the show. One day David said, 'I'm tired of this,' and he took the negative of a film he had just completed—a Burt Reynolds film called *Rough Cut*—to the Chemical Bank and said, 'Here is Burt Reynolds's next picture. I need $2.5 million'—and he got it! In financial circles, it's unheard of for a bank to loan a theatrical producer money like that, but they thought they had gold with *Rough Cut* in the can. As it turned out, it was a bust—a big flop—and *42nd Street* went on to become one of the most profitable musicals of all time."

by Harry Haun

YOUNG AND HEALTHY

Words by
AL DUBIN

Music by
HARRY WARREN

GO INTO YOUR DANCE

Words by
AL DUBIN

Music by
HARRY WARREN

YOU'RE GETTING TO BE A HABIT WITH ME

Words by
AL DUBIN

Music by
HARRY WARREN

I don't know ex-act-ly how it start-ed, but it start-ed in

fun;___ I just want-ed some-one to be gay with, to

GETTING OUT OF TOWN

Words by
MICHAEL STEWART
Original Words by
MORT DIXON and JOE YOUNG

Music by
HARRY WARREN

Moderately fast 2

Verse:

1. I'm wear - ing my hat and coat. ____

I'm leav - ing the cat a note. ____

Quick, call ____ me a fer - ry - boat. ____ Get - ting

hot - cha.

6. My neigh - bors are aw - ful nice._____

To Coda

They've prom - ised to feed the mice. ____

Hey, Ice - man! Don't need your ice. ____ Get - ting

out of town. ____

D. S. 𝄋 al Coda ⊕

Coda

Additional Verses

2. A new kind of company,
   It's just magnetizin' me.
   I'm footloose and fancy free.
   Gettin' out of town.

3. I'm shinin' my travelin' shoes.
   Big scoop in the Daily News.
   "Who's sayin' his toodle-oos?"
   Gettin' out of town.

4. I'm grabbing my hat and coat.
   I'm leaving the cat a note.
   Quick, call me a ferryboat.
   Gettin' out of town.

5. *(Girls)* We're leavin' the boys in style.
   We're linin' 'em up in file,
   And givin' them each a smile.
   Gettin' out of town.

Bridge

Cares fly by. They're sayin' bye, bye,
And we're shoutin', "Hoorah!"
Wings spreadin' 'cause we're headin' for
Hotcha, hotcha, cha, cha.

6. My neighbors are awful nice.
   They've promised to feed the mice.
   Hey, Iceman! Don't need your ice.
   Gettin' out of town.

7. My tickets are in my hand.
   Gosh, isn't the feelin' grand.
   Good gracious, they've sent a band!
   Gettin' out of town.

SHADOW WALTZ

Words by
AL DUBIN

Music by
HARRY WARREN

Shad-ows on the wall, _____ I can see them fall _____ here and there, _____

_____ ev-'ry-where. _____ Sil-hou-ettes in blue, _____ danc-ing in the dew; _____

here am I, _____ where are you? _____

Shadow Waltz - 3 - 1

DAMES

Words by
AL DUBIN

Music by
HARRY WARREN

Dames - 4 - 1

KEEP YOUNG AND BEAUTIFUL

Words by
AL DUBIN

Music by
HARRY WARREN

What's cute a-bout a lit-tle cu-tie? It's her beau-ty, not brains. Old Fath-er Time will nev-er harm you if your

I ONLY HAVE EYES FOR YOU

Words by
AL DUBIN

Music by
HARRY WARREN

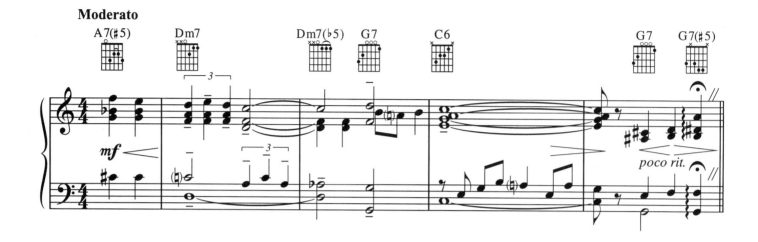

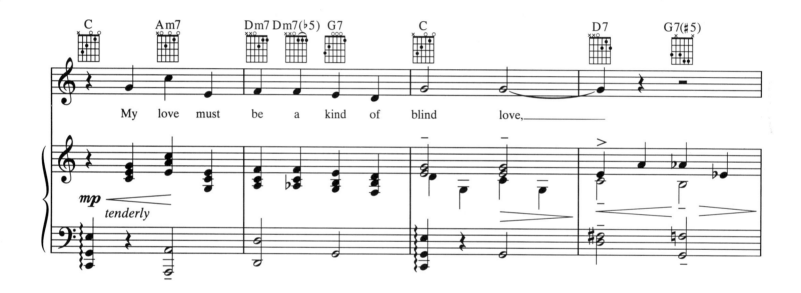

My love must be a kind of blind love, I can't see an-y-one but you.

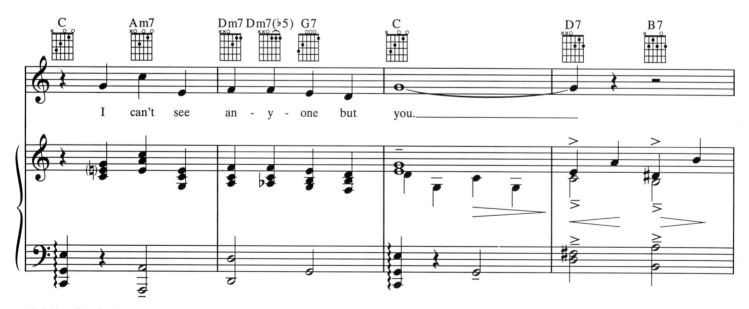

I Only Have Eyes For You - 5 - 1

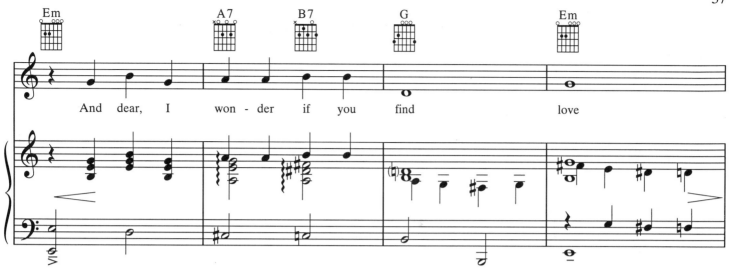

And dear, I won-der if you find love

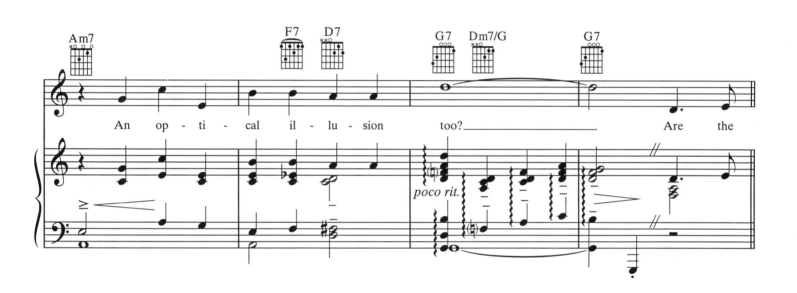

An op-ti-cal il-lu-sion too?_____ Are the

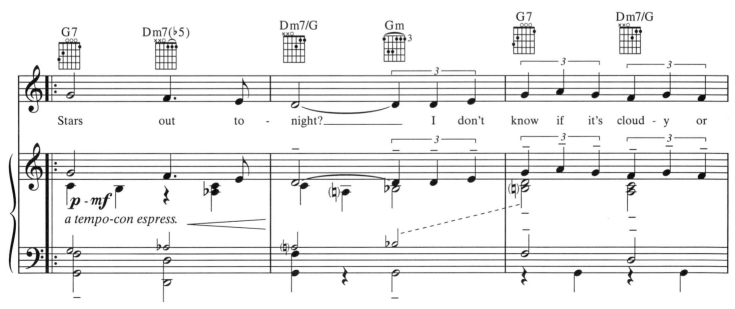

Stars out to - night?_____ I don't know if it's cloud - y or

38

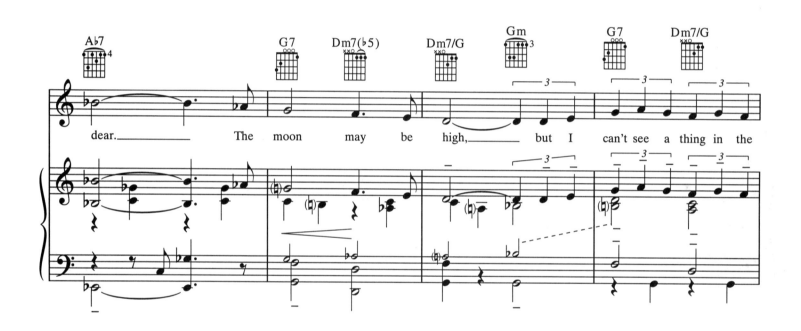

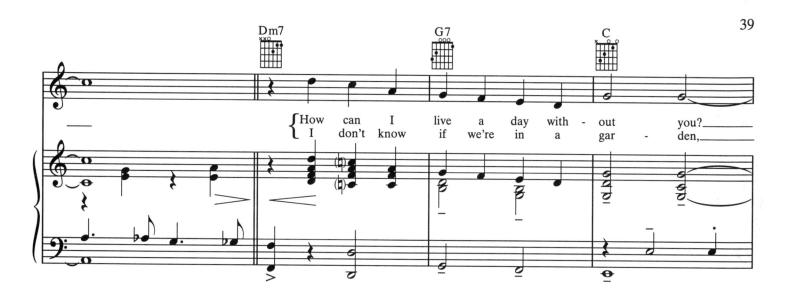

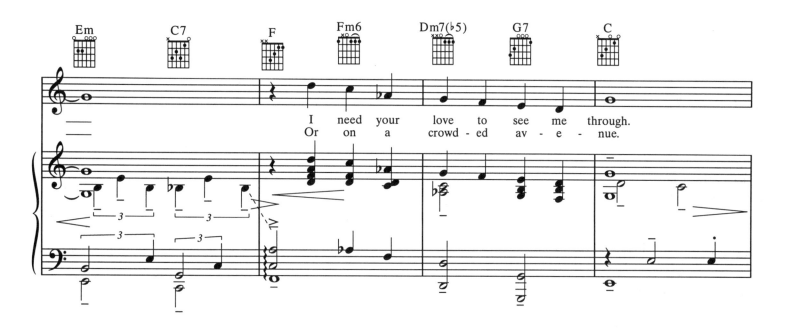

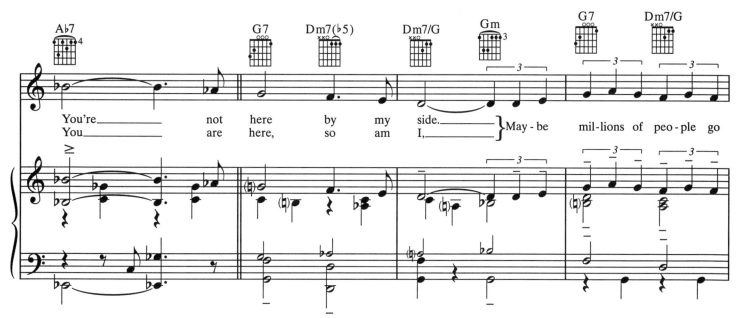

I Only Have Eyes For You - 5 - 4

40

by,_____ But they all dis - ap - pear_____ from

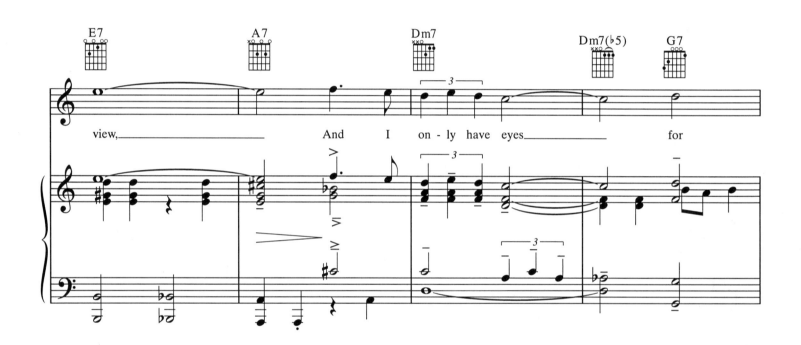

view,_____ And I on - ly have eyes_____ for

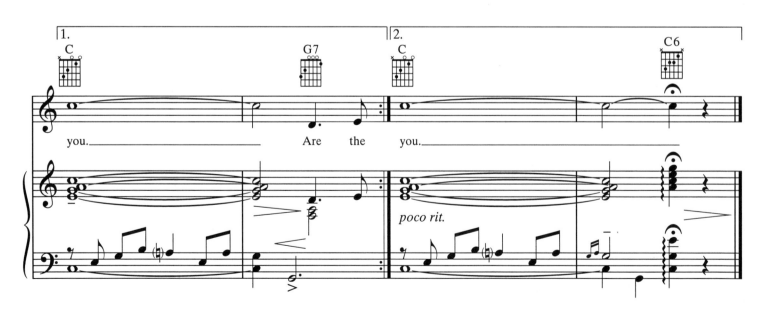

you._____ Are the you._____

THE GOLD DIGGERS' SONG
(We're in the Money)

Words by
AL DUBIN

Music by
HARRY WARREN

Gone are my blues, and gone are my tears; ___

I've got good news to shout in your ears. ___

The sil-ver dol-lar has re-turned to the fold, ___ with

42

THERE'S A SUNNY SIDE
TO EVERY SITUATION

Words by
JOHNNY MERCER

Music by
HARRY WARREN

There's a Sunny Side to Every Situation - 4 - 1

There's a Sunny Side to Every Situation - 4 - 2

WITH PLENTY OF MONEY AND YOU

Words by
AL DUBIN

Music by
HARRY WARREN

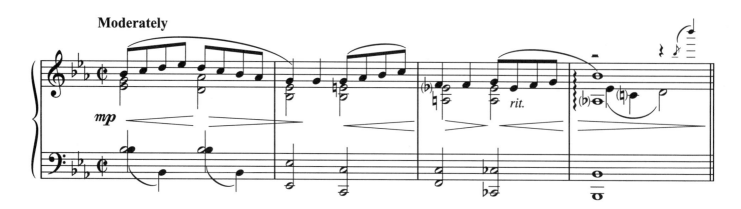

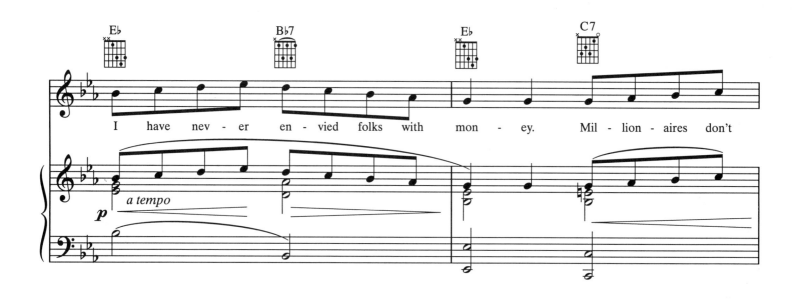

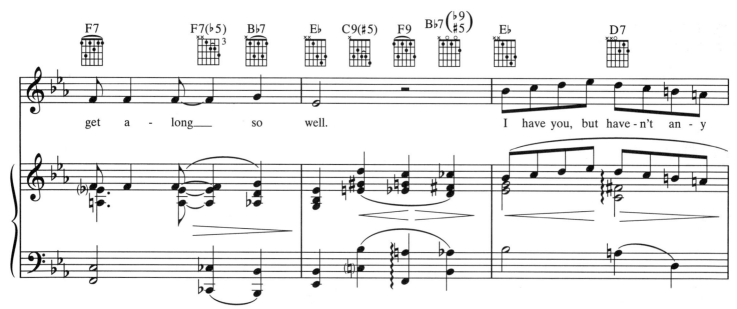

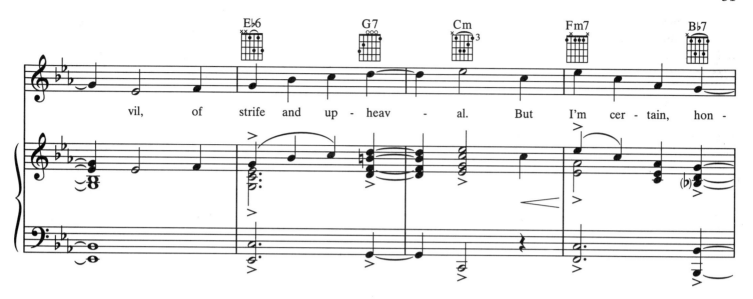

vil, of strife and up-heav - al. But I'm cer-tain, hon -

ey, that life could be sun - ny, with plen-ty of mon -

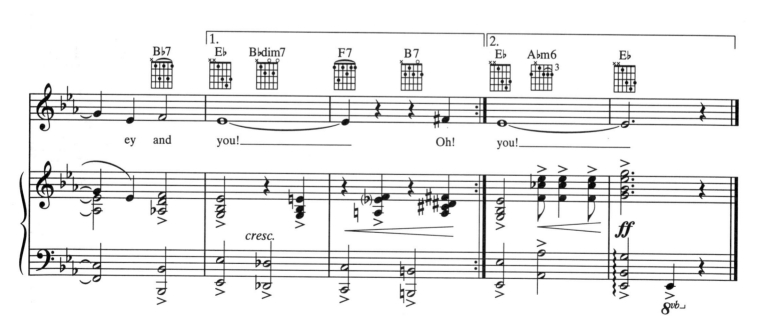

ey and you!_____ Oh! you!_____

cresc.

ff

ABOUT A QUARTER TO NINE

Words by
AL DUBIN

Music by
HARRY WARREN

SHUFFLE OFF TO BUFFALO

Words by
AL DUBIN

Music by
HARRY WARREN

Now that we have had the rice and flow-ers, the knot is tied; I can vis-u-'lize such hap-py hours, __ close by your side. The hon-ey-moon in store is

Shuffle Off to Buffalo - 4 - 1

FORTY-SECOND STREET

Words by
AL DUBIN

Music by
HARRY WARREN

Forty-Second Street - 4 - 1

LULLABY OF BROADWAY

Words by
AL DUBIN

Music by
HARRY WARREN

Lullaby of Broadway - 3 - 1

good - night, milk-man's on his way.___ Sleep

tight, Ba - by, sleep tight,

1. let's call it a day,___ Hey!___ 2. Let's call it a day.___

Lis - ten to the lul - la - by of old Broad - way.___

Michael Arnold and Company

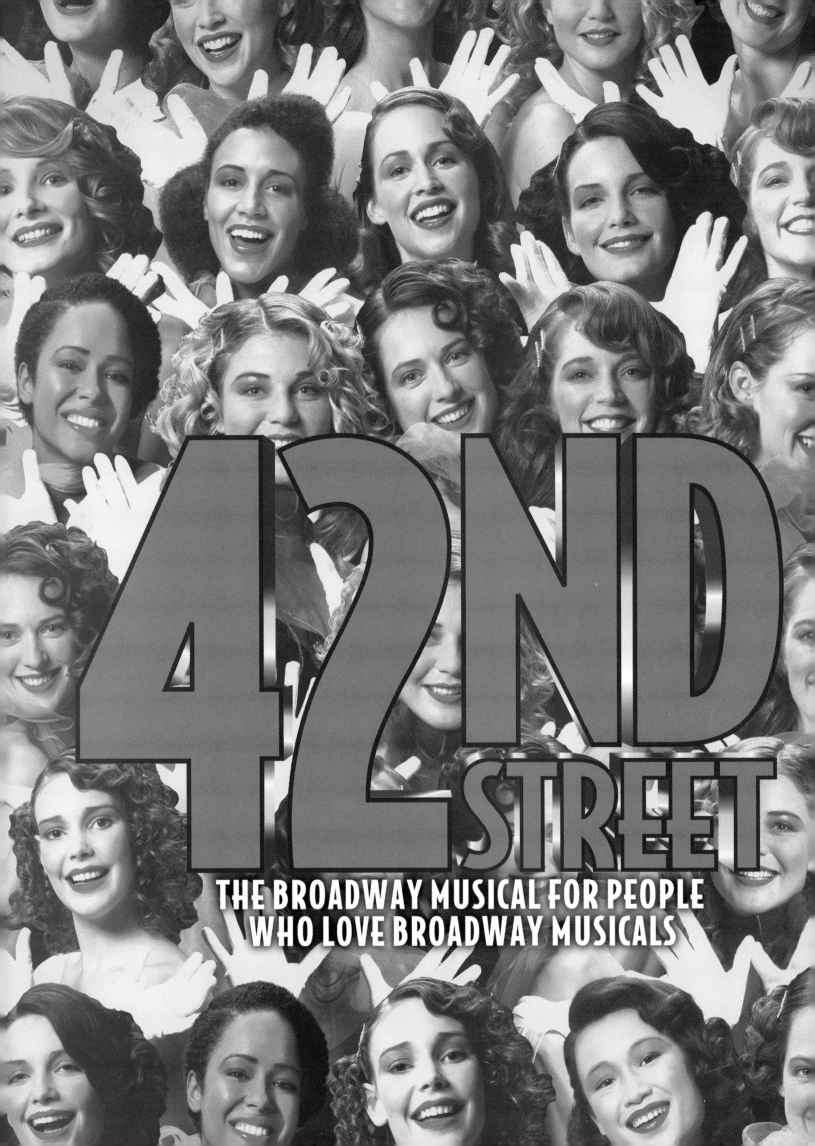

42ND STREET

THE BROADWAY MUSICAL FOR PEOPLE WHO LOVE BROADWAY MUSICALS